MAINTAINING
BALANCE

*a motivational guide to a
simple self-discovery process
that will transform your life*

DR. MICKEL ANGLIN

Printed in the United States of America

ISBN: 978-0-692-18169-0

MY GRATITUDE

B*efore diving into the core of this guide,* I want to take the time to thank my true savior, my God. My life has not been a fairy tale. I give my God all praise for all things. He has saved me, transformed me, and restored me. He constantly works on my life path, which has made me the man I am today. Even though I am not perfect, I am grateful for a second chance and for what lies ahead in my future.

Next, I thank my wife. My forgiving partner and trusted friend who has been by my side during my transformation. God knew whom he was sending me, at the right time, at the right moment, and at the right stage in my life. She serves as a backbone for me as I learn about myself.

I am grateful my parents had the vision to bring us to the United States. They knew that boundaries would evaporate in this great country. They had the courage to pack up their lives and bring four kids and six suitcases to the United States and start over.

Lastly, I thank my kids. In this guide I hope to deliver

advice for them to live by and use throughout their lives. I pray that they won't go down some of the paths I chose and hope they use my thoughts as a beacon and a guide for their lives.

INTRODUCTION

t's important to me that I show up. Daily. In everything that I do, in everything that I say, and in every action that I take. Do I live by these words every day? In the past, no. In the present, yes (most days—I'm not perfect).

It's not that easy when you have the responsibilities of a being a private practice doctor, NFL team physician, business owner, husband, father, brother, friend, and son. With so many things pulling me in different directions, life could consume and overwhelm me, making joy fleeting and bitterness constant. But it shouldn't be that way. I wanted to be eager to get up every day, not hit *snooze* and bury my head under my pillow.

Being a doctor gives me numerous opportunities to counsel people when they need it most. In those who listen, I see transformations. They get pep back in their step. I love seeing that. It's a great feeling. No. It's the best feeling.

Over the years I have realized I have a formula to help people lead balanced lives. It's what we need. Balanced lives open doors. Open doors provide opportunities. Opportunities fulfill dreams. Answered dreams bring happiness. I've done it, and I want you to have the chance to do the same.

This guide will give you the tools to transform your life. Use it as your footing and jump off.

CONTENTS

> A life that displays my *who* and my *why* with the ultimate focus on a healthy balance.

CHAPTER ONE

SETTING THE STAGE

Who I am and what my purpose is

Throughout life, if you are anything like me, you will have many questions. And you will have many problems.

I often ask about life's design, and about my purpose and place on this journey. As I age and accept learned wisdom, I have made it my passion to search for the answer to what I believe is the most essential question, "How can I live a balanced, full, joyful and purpose-driven life?" A life that is enriching and rewarding. A life that displays my *who* and my *why* with the ultimate focus on a healthy balance.

In this guide, I will share with you my thoughts, ideas, and paths to achieve that balance. I will explore and define how to live life right and how to do it daily with "grind and grit." I pray that my thoughts will serve as a pathway and guide for living life the way it should be, with a daily script.

Before you read any further, I encourage you to ask yourself the following questions:

1. What is important to you?
2. What makes you?
3. Who do you believe in?

These central questions define who we are, what we do, and how we do it.

CHAPTER TWO

LIFE IS A VERB

> 66
>
> Life, in its rawest essence,
> means you are in the
> constant act of doing.
>
> 99

O*ften, as a physician, I get asked some simple questions:* "Why is life so hard, Doc?" "Do you have any suggestions on how to make this thing we call life an easier experience?" "Do you have any hints or tips you can share with me to make it better?"

In the beginning stages of my career, I struggled with these questions because I was trying to find the right answers. But now, with my own past failures, trials, and triumphs, I have come to the realization that there is not a simple answer or solution.

The reality is life can be hard, but it also can be REALLY GOOD. Life will have its ups and downs—tears of failure and joys of victory. When we realize this, we find there are more than just one or two or three answers. There is not just one concrete pathway or solution. We realize that life is in constant motion and constant action. Life is truly a VERB. Life, in its rawest essence, means you are in the constant act of doing.

To illustrate this concept, I would like to share with you one of the many lessons my kids have taught me as I grow in relationship with them. One day my then-four-year-old son approached his mom and asked her if she and I would help him build a robot friend. Not just any old friend but a robot friend. In his simple and innocent mind, he figured that if we used a grocery store paper bag with various arts and crafts supplies, we would be able to create this terrific masterpiece.

Now, at the time of his approach, my wife was in the middle of cooking dinner and I was conversing casually with her. My four-year-old knew that this robot friend-building was not going to occur at this very moment. But that did not stop him. He talked on and on about the "end result" of having his new friend.

He imagined how he and his new friend would be best buddies and play together. Eat together. Sleep together. Even go to school together. After imagining and verbalizing these very intense and detailed future life experiences, he then ran off to our hall closet to pick out what he thought would be all the essential supplies and tools needed to construct his robot friend. Among them were scissors, paper, glue, crayons, hats, paper clips, and even a pair of socks. He had it all figured out. As I watched him run back and forth, his eyes lit up. His smile was as wide as the ocean and his heart was content and full of joy.

Finally, the moment came when my wife finished making dinner and we all headed upstairs to his room to make his robot. The task was simple. My wife focused on all the major details of the robot friend, including the head, hair, eyes, mouth, chest, and arms. My son's only task was to make his legs. My task was to supervise (watch two people I truly love "do life"). As I watched the process, I observed once again this little and very cute four-year-old's eyes lighting up with happiness radiating from his very being. He was loving every bit of the journey as he created his robot friend. While he made, from his perspective, the best set of legs for his future buddy, he continued to talk about the life they were going to have together and the memories they would make.

At last, after about an hour, my four-year-old son's new friend was complete. He looked great! He was a little wobbly but appeared perfect to my son. That night, his robot friend ate dinner with us and even got the chance to sleep in the bed with him. In the days that followed, he played less and less with his robot, until one day, the robot was relegated to a dark corner—essentially to nonexistence. You see, as is customary with most four-years old kids, our son's life had moved on. He had moved on to bigger and better ideas, toys, and imaginings. However, one thing has not moved on to this day. When our four-year-old was asked about his robot friend stashed away in the corner, he could vividly remember and tell the story about the day he made a paper robot with his parents.

So, what is the point? We cannot get wrapped up in the "end result". We cannot obsess about trying to solve the problem right now. We cannot get bogged down in trying to live the perfect life. There is no magic formula. We must enjoy the process. Enjoy the act of doing. Enjoy the act of being a great student, a great parent, a great working professional, a great friend, a great whatever your heart desires.

As we dive deeper into this guide and explore the art of living a balanced life, my hope for us all is that we can truly live an amazingly awesome and balanced life. That we can enjoy the process and journey, just like a four-year-old.

CHAPTER THREE

THE FOUNDATIONAL PILLARS

Faith.
Family.
Future.
Fitness.

> ❝
> Never be too scared to pivot your future.
> ❞

*n life, there are four **Foundational** areas that I believe are necessary to maintain balance.* These are faith, family, future, and fitness.

NUMBER ONE IS YOUR FAITH. You must believe that you are not here by chance. You must believe that you were created by someone greater than you for a greater purpose. My faith is everything! My faith reminds me that I am a child of a higher being and He who created me did not make me by chance. My creator is supreme. Without this belief, nothing else matters. I have an abundant faith that my creator has a purpose for my life and I was created to serve. I have faith that our time on this planet Earth, although brief in the big picture of eternal life, plays a vital role.

It is our responsibility to do something that's worth something. We must aspire to be someone who has credibility, someone with passion and purpose, someone who will play his or her role in helping humanity. My faith is strong because I am proof that there is a creator that has full control of our lives. My creator has saved me countless times from self-destruction and has picked me up from the lowest points of life when I felt there was no end in sight.

Despite my transgressions, my creator has allowed me to be a physician and has blessed me with a platform of influence to help and heal people mentally, physically, and spiritually. My faith, through the concept of reciprocity, teaches me right from wrong and to treat others with kindness, respect, and love.

NUMBER TWO IS YOUR FAMILY. To understand the *Foundational Pillar* of family you don't have to be married or have kids. We all come from someone and we all are a part of a family, biological or not. Life without a focus on family can be hard. We need a person or persons in our lives during our daily grind to be there for support, love, laughter, and comfort. Family reminds you to work hard each day, holds you accountable, and challenges you to be the best version of yourself every day.

Family reminds you to have a limitless career and no boundaries. Family reminds you to be a good role model and to aspire to success and humility. When I succeed I give my wife and kids the comfort, provision, and protection they deserve.

When I succeed, I give my kids a role model and guide

to help them be prepared for all of life's many challenges and victories. When I succeed I give my parents the satisfaction of knowing they made the right choice to emigrate to the United States, despite the many weary nights and grindingly difficult days. Having a focus on family reminds me that if I were to fail, I not only would fail myself, but also my family. It is this focus on family that makes failing not an option.

NUMBER THREE IS YOUR FUTURE. The *Foundational Pillar* of future defines our careers. What we do for a living. My future gets me up early and it is why I study hard. It is because of my focus on my future that I went to school with a purpose of earning good grades and doing well academically. My future motivated me to join various organizations and become involved in community-wide activities. My future pushed me to strengthen my résumé, apply to the best colleges and pursue the best scholarships.

Focusing on my future inspired me to study when everyone else was partying. Your future is your source. Your future is your resource. Your future dictates how you provide for yourself and your family. Keeping your future in proper balance is essential. Most of our days will in some way involve our future. Choose this pillar in life well. Take the time to envision yourself five, ten, or fifteen years out and what it is you want to be doing.

Sculpt your future every day. Analyze your future and adapt your future as you evolve. Never be scared to pivot your future. No matter what, stay true to yourself and your life goals and make every attempt to align your goals, purposes, and passions with your future.

THE LAST *Foundational Pillar* IS FITNESS. This should drive your everyday script in life. Not just physical fitness but also mental fitness. Unfortunately, this is an area that many of us take for granted. We all tend to focus on everything else—our jobs, our finances, our relationships. We forget to make our own self a priority.

As I have grown older and matured, a huge life lesson I am learning is simply this: if you do not feel good, you're not going to do well. Simple as that. If you do not feel good, you will not do well. On the contrary, if you feel good, you will do well and most of the time you will do your best. As I have shared with my kids, in life there is no room for shortcuts or sloppiness. When you become sloppy, do sloppy work, and take shortcuts, you will not reach your goals. This also applies to your body and your mind.

When you focus on your physical fitness you become deliberate about what you eat, how much you eat, when you exercise, and how much you exercise. Physical fitness also requires getting the proper amount of sleep so that you have bounding energy to go that extra mile when your body says no!

Mental fitness means disciplining your life to protect every aspect of your mind and mental being. You will fail when your mind is not fit. You will fall short when there is a mental breakdown. Guard and protect your mind. Keep it fit today and maintain the fitness of your mind to endure for tomorrow.

CHAPTER FOUR

THE
PARADIGMS

Personal.
Professional.
Psychological.
Physical.
Personality.

"

Your mind is your steering wheel.
It will dictate the path you take
toward your destiny.

"

o now you know and understand what the important
areas in your life should be: faith, family, future, and
fitness. You may now dive further into what I call the
Paradigms. A paradigm is a standard, perspective, or set of
ideas. A paradigm is a way of looking at something. There are
five areas of life that you will want to work on every day, every
second, every minute. The **Paradigms** become your blueprint
for life. They become your roadmap for your everyday journey.
In life, you must envision where you want to go before making
the first step.

With all the hustle and bustle of everyday life, we often get caught up in our daily chores, our daily responsibilities, the daily demands on us. And often this ritual is one of negativity. One that instantaneously gives us stress, heartache, and turmoil. Thoughts about having to go the same job that we do not like, having to take the long traffic-ridden commute to our kid's school and work, or having to deal with co-workers we do not particularly like or a boss who does not appreciate us or a spouse who has emotionally checked out.

These daily rituals will spoil your mind, rob you of happiness, and ultimately destroy your joy. So, it is imperative that every day you take control and command of your why and your purpose for that day. Just waking up is NOT enough. Mentally, you must align and arrange the **Paradigms** for your day. The five areas of life that need your attention EVERY day are *personal, professional, psychological, physical, and personality.*

THE FIRST *Paradigm* IS YOUR PERSONAL LIFE. You should work on your personal life every day. Be the best person and version of yourself you can be. The personal paradigm is the first and most important paradigm because it ties into all the **Foundational Pillars.** When you look into the mirror you see the only person on this Earth who ultimately will define how you think about yourself.

You need to tell yourself that you are loved. Tell yourself that you were created for a purpose. Tell yourself that this day was created uniquely for you and that your path will lead you to a place of significance, not only for your life but for someone else as well. This affirmation needs to happen every day. Your personal paradigm is strongly predicated upon your faith pillar and your foundational belief system, so choose it well.

Take time every day to reflect on your present core self and your ideal core self. Simply put, who are you right now and who is it you want to be? Who made you? And always In a POSITIVE way, try and imagine WHY? What will you do today to be the person YOU want to be? The personal paradigm ties directly into how you see yourself in your family, whether it is the family you are from or the family you are creating, or both. The choices you make each day will affect these interpersonal relationships so please be intentional about your choices.

REMEMBER, no one is perfect, but we can all strive to be perfect, EVERY DAY. The personal paradigm ties into your future. The person you are in your job dictates your attitude and longevity. If you focus on staying in balance in your personal life, the rewards will follow. You will climb in your career and achieve your goals.

Lastly and most importantly, the personal paradigm heavily relies on your fitness, mental and physical. Every day, you must have an action plan to tap into these two dimensions. Your mind is your steering wheel. It will dictate the path you take toward your destiny. CONTROL your mind and you CONTROL your destiny. A clear mind is a light unto thy path. Make room in the beginning, middle, and end of your days to clear your mind to maintain mental fitness.

Likewise, and very similarly, the fitness **Foundational Pillar** plays a major role in your personal paradigm. Take care of your body. Just a little a day is all that is needed. Rehearsing and recording this process will become a habit that not only balances you but ultimately makes you feel good about yourself.

THE SECOND IS YOUR PROFESSIONAL LIFE. Often this paradigm gets misaligned. We often fall into the trap of "just doing." We say to ourselves, "It is just a job." Or "It is what puts food on the table." Or "This is how I provide for my family." That is not TRUE of the professional *Paradigm.* Do not get me wrong; there is nothing wrong with being responsible and taking care of yourself and your family with a job or any commitment. As a matter of fact, especially these days, people often take advantage of the system and live their lives always being the victim. I truly commend and applaud anyone willing to take charge of his or her own life by having a job.

However, my challenge for us all is to not let every day be just about the daily grind of providing. Take some time in your days to do what you truly love and what fulfills your purpose, even if it is just for a small moment, second, or minute. Try and align yourself with work that makes you BURN! A profession that leaks through your very pores the greatness within you and unleashes your God-given talents. A career that creates significance for those around you. Please, please, do not fall into the trap of thinking that you must be a doctor, lawyer, or engineer to do this. Do not fall into the trap of thinking that you must be rich to do this.

Your true calling will be yours because it is you. No one and nothing can take that from you. Your influence on this great universe can be tapped as a mailman, a mom, a tax collector, or a janitor. Whatever your calling is, just do it WELL. Leave your imprint every day and do it all over again the next day.

THE THIRD *Paradigm* IS THE PSYCHOLOGICAL PARADIGM.
This particular paradigm draws from the **Foundational Pillar**
of faith and fitness. Balance begins in your mind. Your heart,
your body, and your soul are all very important elements of what
makes you, but it is your mind that steers the ship. It shapes your
outlook, your perspective, and your attitudes in life.

Without psychological balance, your whole life will be out of
sync. Your journey through life will be threatened each day with
derailment. Psychological balance allows you to stay the course
and feel alive. If you truly want to maintain balance, you must
maintain your psyche.

So, with thought, with devotion, with meditation, and
with reflection, map out your thoughts and achieve a sense of
peace for the day. This will allow you to set the boundaries of
your daily emotions, responses, and reactions. Life will throw
curveballs, both big and small, but with a "thought plan" you are
less likely to react in ways that you will regret.

End your day with some sort of activity to promote physical
fitness. A healthy and active body soothes the mind. A fit body,
or even the attempt to make your body fit, allows the mind to
breathe, to vent, and to restore. If you master the practice of
mental and physical fitness, the psychological paradigm will
be in focus, it will be balanced, and you will soar through the
journey of life, no matter what.

THE FOURTH *Paradigm* IS PHYSICAL. The physical paradigm
obviously draws from the foundational pillar of fitness. Also,

as I previously alluded to, it as an integral component of your psychological paradigm. But it is such an important ingredient that I feel it is necessary to emphasize it as a separate paradigm. You need to be physically ready for the daily grind. You must be physically ready to tackle all the craziness of life. Life is not easy and probably never will be. You must have physical (as well as mental) endurance to win the race.

To succeed in life, you need not be strong, tall, mighty, or smart. No, the race is won by the one who endures. Simply, if you are not in good physical shape and ready for the long haul, you will get tired; you will want to quit, or even worse, you will blame others for your shortcomings. Understanding this key "secret sauce" will push you to guard your temple, your body, the great epicenter of what stores "you."

Pay attention to what you put in your body, what you drink, what you eat, and yes, how much rest you are giving it to allow it to restore. Be physically fit. Make it your intention every day to chip away at getting closer to having a body that will endure and last.

LASTLY, THE FIFTH *Paradigm* IS YOUR PERSONALITY. Your personality reflects your attitude toward life. Yes, we all have different personalities; some of us are extroverts and some are introverts. Whichever you are, the personality I am referring to here illuminates your natural self and reaches for the supernatural. Both extroverts and introverts will have bad days, say the wrong things, and react to the pressures of life in ways they will later regret.

However, every day we can make it an intentional focus to

strive for a personality that lights up any room, any atmosphere, any situation. By nature, I am an introvert, but daily I make it my mission and goal to be a personal, social, and professional extrovert. This should be your goal as well. As was once said by the great Les Brown, "You are either coming or you're going." You are either saying hello or goodbye.

Make it a focus to be the person with the personality that says loudly, "I AM COMING AND HELLO!" If you do, positive things will happen to you. The stratosphere will gravitate toward you and bring along opportunities you would never have imagined. Bad will become good and good will become great. Practice a positive personality and the way you look at the world and the way the world looks at you will never be the same.

The **Paradigms** of your life are your roadmap. They will guide your every step and intention toward your goals for the day and for life. Practice them and focus on them daily to attain the healthy balance that is necessary to successfully live the verb that is life.

How does one do this? Here is my learned wisdom that I will encourage you to practice each and every day. Practice mental fitness in the morning and physical fitness in the evening. Simply, start your day!

CHAPTER FIVE

THE DAILY SCRIPT

**Scripture.
Source.
Study.
Sculpture.
Satisfaction.**

"

Reflection and meditation open channels that
flow unblocked by yesterday's concerns,
yesterday's troubles, and yesterday's fears.

"

*W*hen you understand your true core values and can
identify the **Foundational Pillars** of life that matter
to you as a human being, you can then open yourself
to explore and nourish the key **Paradigms** of life. The roadmap
to our journey has been drawn and now it is time to act.

How? When? At what rhythm? At what cadence? The
answers to the next step flow naturally by following what I
have termed "living out our daily script." Your daily plan is
your journey that taps into all your self-identified paradigms
and pillars. With a daily script or routine that is based on your

wishes, wants, and whys, you leave no room for imbalance. No room for error. Practicing a daily script feeds the development of a healthy and balanced life.

THE FIRST DAILY *Script* STARTS YOUR DAY OFF WITH SCRIPTURE. Spend your first seconds, minutes, or even hour of your day reading scripture. The scripture I am referring to does not have to be biblical or religious; it can be a word or verse or simply a message that focuses your mind on positive thinking and a healthy mindset. Reflection and meditation open channels that flow unblocked by yesterday's concerns, yesterday's troubles, and yesterday's fears. Start each day fresh with a sense of gratitude, of hope and peace. Every day is a gift and an opportunity for new beginnings. Intentionally meditating on a positive scripture sets you up for life anew.

THE SECOND DAILY *Script* FOR LIVING A BALANCED LIFE IS YOUR SOURCE. The source script brings into focus your career and profession. It is indeed our source that provides for our daily needs. Focus on it well. Never let a day go by without giving your source 126 percent. Display, influence, and share your God-given talents with the world. Most of your day is spent in this space so I urge you to do it well. Appreciate every day that your ability to do the job you do is a gift. Never be complacent.

Always strive to reach for more, accomplish more, and give back more. Make your source in life an enrichment for whoever touches it, whatever line it crosses, and wherever it takes you. Practicing this level of discipline in your source will reward you with happiness and success.

THE THIRD DAILY *Script* **FOR LIVING A BALANCED LIFE IS STUDY.** Your study equals your knowledge. Never lose your hunger to learn more about your craft. Enrich your mind daily with new knowledge, new ideas, and new solutions. Take the time during your day to challenge yourself. Make yourself uncomfortable. Allow your thoughts and your insights to be comfortable with being uncomfortable. The adage "you lose what you do not use" applies to all areas of your life, but especially to your body and even more specifically to your mind. Push your limits with new hopes and creations.

THE FOURTH DAILY *Script* **FOR LIVING A BALANCED LIFE IS SCULPTURE.** Sculpture is physically exercising every day and sculpting your body as you endure the verb of life. Often people put this part of life off because it can be one of the most overwhelming challenges to face. We tend to run away from this because it is the easiest part of our life plan to let go. No one will make you exercise or sculpt your body. No one will challenge you to get into the best physical shape you can.

NO. You must challenge yourself. You and you alone must do this. Make it a habit. Take the first steps—literally. A five-minute walk today, a ten-minute run tomorrow, and so on. Don't plan to climb to the top of the mountain in one day. Have fun with it. Do what you like. Make it a habit. The rewards of daily physical activity will balance you not only physically but also mentally. Sculpting your body draws from your fitness pillar and your psychological, personal, and physical Paradigms, leading you to a healthy, full, and balanced life.

LASTLY, THE FIFTH DAILY *Script* FOR LIVING A BALANCED LIFE IS SATISFACTION. When you end each day with satisfaction, you bring life all back together. All pillars and all paradigms in life need the element of satisfaction. Otherwise, what is the purpose? Reward yourself with healthy and PURE habits, actions, and routines that allow you to be satisfied.

Restore your mind, body, and soul with the satisfaction it needs to do it all over again tomorrow. Spend time with your family. Spend time with your significant other. Spend time with your friends. Spend time with yourself. Check in to your relationships and with the people who care about you. Check in with yourself. Satisfy and restore your life today for the grind that is coming tomorrow.

CHAPTER SIX

BALANCE IS THE ART OF OVERCOMING YOUR BREAKING POINT

Putting it all together

> ""
> If you are near your breaking point,
> something IS off balance.
> ""

After you put it all together by defining your **Foundation Pillars,** establishing your **Paradigms,** and living out your daily **Script,** you will gain a new understanding. You realize that life is not about any one thing or doing one task but rather about the balancing act that prevents you from passing your breaking point.

Balance is the art of overcoming your breaking point. At some point in our life, each of us will reach or almost reach our breaking point. If you have not yet, you will. Expect it. Own it. Learn from it but never pass it. Never let it keep you down.

Keep getting back up. Look around. Analyze. Observe. Reflect. If you are near your breaking point, something IS off balance. Take time and just simply step back. Put your life back in balance. Redefine your **Foundation Pillars,** redesign your **Paradigms,** and start your daily **Script** over.

Just remember, maintaining balance is the art of overcoming your breaking point.

MAINTAINING
BALANCE
...Through it all

THE **F**OUNDATIONAL PILLARS
- **F**aith
- **F**amily
- **F**uture
- **F**itness

THE **P**ARADIGMS
- **P**ersonal
- **P**rofessional
- **P**sychological
- **P**hysical
- **P**ersonality

THE DAILY **S**CRIPT
- **S**cripture
- **S**ource
- **S**tudy
- **S**atisfaction
- **S**culpture